ULTIMATE ADVENTURE SPORTS
ROCK CLIMBING
- EXCLUSIVE -

AUTHOR
SALLY WARREN

Redback Publishing

PO Box 357, Frenchs Forest, NSW 2086, Australia

www.redbackpublishing.com
orders@redbackpublishing.com

© Redback Publishing 2023

ISBN 978-1-922322-97-5 HBK

All rights reserved. No part of this publication may be reproduced in any form or by any means (including photocopying or storing it in any medium by electronic means and whether or not transiently or incidentally to some other use of this publication) without the written permission of the copyright owner. Applications for the copyright owner's written permission should be addressed to the publisher.

Author: Sally Warren
Editor: Caroline Thomas
Designer: Redback Publishing

Original illustrations:
© Redback Publishing 2023
Originated by Redback Publishing

Printed and bound in Malaysia

Acknowledgements
Abbreviations: l—left, r—right, b—bottom, t—top,
c—centre, m—middle
We would like to thank the following for permission to reproduce photographs:
(Images © Shutterstock) P05br by Golden_Bura, p96bl Chinese artist(s) from the 10th century, Public domain, via Wikimedia Common, p7tl Swi 688.59, Houghton Library, Harvard University, p24 AO Production via Wikimedia, p24tr Pavel Blazek via Wikimedia, p25tl Rachel Jackson via Flickr, p25tr Goat_VSH via Flickr, p30tl by Alex Brylov, p30bl&r by gubernat.

Disclaimer
Every effort has been made to contact copyright holders of any material reproduced in this book. Any omissions will be rectified in subsequent printings if notice is given to the publisher.

A catalogue record for this book is available from the National Library of Australia

CONTENTS

What is Rock Climbing? **4**
Brief History **6**
Where do People Climb? **8**
Learning to Rock Climb **10**
Disciplines Within the Sport **12**
What is Abseiling? **14**
What About Ice Climbing? **16**
Grading System **18**
Knots for Climbing **20**
Extra Equipment and Clothing **22**
Professional Rock Climbers **24**
Indoor Rock Climbing **26**
Dangers of the Sport **28**
Rock Climbing Events **30**
Glossary **31**
Index **32**

WOW!

EPIC ADVENTURE AWAITS!

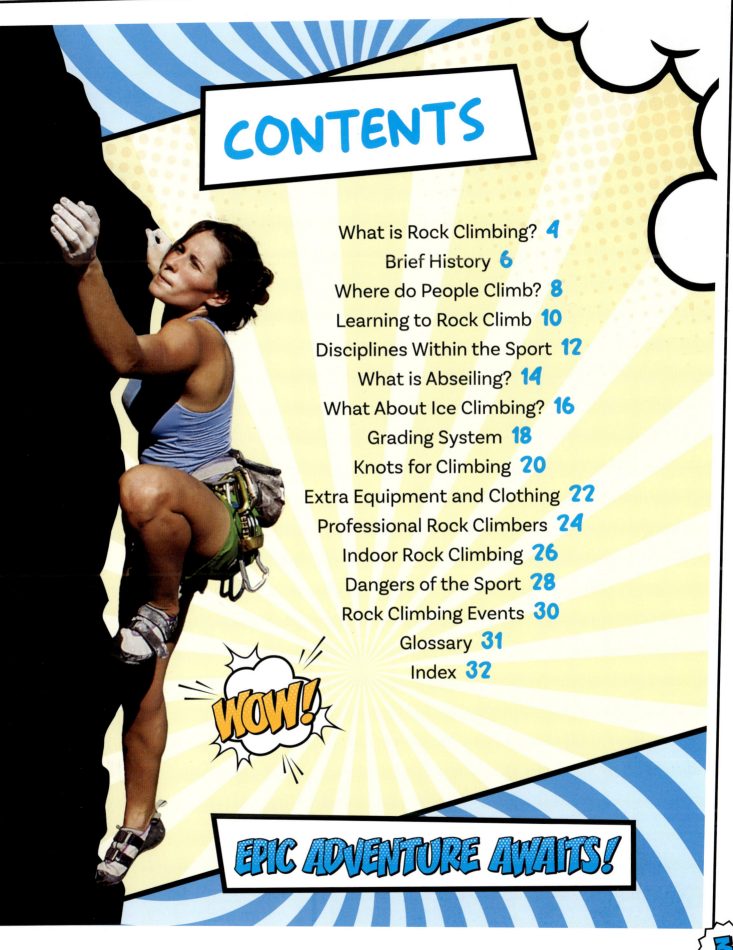

WHAT IS ROCK CLIMBING?

Are rock climbers insane? What drives them to scale dizzying heights just for fun?

Guess what? It IS super fun! Let's break it down ...

Rock climbing involves climbing up, down or across a rock face, usually following a particular route.

Climbing has amazing health benefits and is both physically and mentally challenging. It is super social, hugely empowering and requires great skill mastery, strength and finesse.

The best thing about climbing is that you are completely present in the moment. This often leads to a feeling of exhilaration and achievement. Above all, it's MEGA fun!

COOL STUFF

Sport Climbing made its Olympic debut at the 2021 Summer Games in Tokyo, Japan. This was the first time in history that the sport was celebrated with a three-part competition, which included speed climbing, bouldering and lead climbing.

BRIEF HISTORY

Climbing has been around since the dawn of time, allowing people to reach safety, resources and even enlightenment. In the days of early civilisations and emerging belief systems, mountains were seen as holy and as a place to be closer to God.

Today, people climb to challenge themselves, feel a sense of accomplishment and trigger the excitement-hormone adrenaline which releases feel-good hormones, endorphins!

Rock climbing has evolved over the years, but is it pure genius, simple madness or utter awesomeness!?

TIMELINE

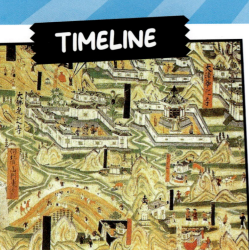

400 BC Paintings were discovered on the ceilings of caves in China. These would have been impossible to paint without climbing up the walls!

1492 The first recorded climber, Antoine de Ville, climbed a 300-metre rock monolith in France. Using tactics developed for sieging castles, his King had hoped he would find flying Angels near its summit. There were no Angels, but a large flower meadow covering the top of the rock!

1857 The first climbing club was founded. It was called the Alpine Club.

1880 The UK officially recognised rock climbing as a sport as W. P. Haskett Smith, known as the Father of Rock Climbing, became a national phenomenon for climbing the Napes Needle in 1886

1914 Free climbing began to emerge – without the use of any protective equipment!

1989 Climbers competed in the first International Climbing World Cup.

2021 Climbing joined the Tokyo Olympics for the first time in history.

WHERE DO PEOPLE CLIMB?

Rock climbing is accessible all over the world, both indoors and outdoors! By far, Yosemite Valley in the USA is one of the most renowned climbing spots in the world, often referred to as the 'Centre of the Universe' by hardcore climbers.

WOW – THIS IS EPIC!

Hanshellaren Cave in Flatanger, Norway boasts the hardest sport-climb in the world. Nick-named 'Silence', the 45-metre route is EXTREME and, so far, has only been completed by the world's best rock climber, Adam Ondra.

SOME OF THE COOLEST SPOTS TO CLIMB

SQUAMISH
Canada

DOLOMITES
Italy

FONTAINEBLEAU
France

KALYMNOS
Greece

TONSAI
Thailand

THE BLUE MOUNTAINS
Australia

LEARNING TO ROCK CLIMB

Guess what? Anyone can rock climb!

All you need is a pair of good climbing shoes, a harness, a few pieces of gear and a friend who is as equally crazy as you are! Remember, safety always (ALWAYS!) comes first! Beyond that, there are no rules for learning to climb. It just depends on how you want to do it.

HERE ARE SOME WAYS TO GET INVOLVED

INDOOR GYMS

Honing your skills and building up strength in a controlled, safe environment is an excellent way to start rock climbing. You can mingle with other climbers, get your lingo sorted out and chat about the best places to go climbing in the area.

EXPERIENCED FRIENDS

Many people start out on their first climb with an experienced climber friend who can literally show them the ropes! This is a great way to learn about equipment and technique and also a fun day out in nature with friends.

CERTIFIED CLIMBING COURSE

There are lots of climbing courses or outdoor education specialists around. You can contact local climbing organisations or gyms to see if they are instructing or running any classes that you can join.

SELF EDUCATION

Just remember safety always (ALWAYS!) comes first! Make sure both you and your partner know the ropes and have your safety knowledge and equipment covered before heading out. Then, it's time to get out to the crag to put your knowledge into action!

DISCIPLINES WITHIN THE SPORT

Rock climbing is rock climbing, right? Wrong! There are many ways to scale a rock face and each requires its own special skill-set.

SPORT CLIMBING

All sport climbs use artificially bolted steel loops that are drilled and glued into the wall. The rope is fed out from a belayer at the bottom of the crag and the climber clips into the bolts as they move up.

TOP ROPING

Generally, new rock climbers begin climbing using a system called Top Roping. Top Ropes are set up before the climber begins, by looping a rope through an anchor at the top of the climb. One end of this rope is tied into your harness and the other end is tied to your belayer (or partner) who stays on the ground below.

BOULDERING

Bouldering means climbing a big chunk of rock or a boulder without ropes, a harness or any bolts – all you need is shoes and chalk. Boulderers usually climb at low heights, so a mat or pad placed underneath is usually enough to break any falls or soften their dismount. Boulderers climb rock 'problems' that require technical skill, balance, flexibility and strength.

TRAD CLIMBING

Traditional or 'trad' climbing was the standard form of climbing before artificially bolted sport routes came about. Trad climbing means finding your own route, rather than following the bolts. Trad climbers carry specialised devices that they wedge into rock crevices to create their own bolt points as they go. These cams, nuts, chocks, wedges and pins are removed as the climber progresses along their route.

FREE SOLOING

A very small proportion of climbers climb Free Solo. This means climbing the full height of a crag without the use of ropes or a harness. A fall when free soloing can be deadly!

WHAT IS ABSEILING?

How on earth do you get back down to the bottom of a cliff after you've climbed up!? Or, so you can climb up in the first place!? That's where abseiling comes in handy.

Rock climbers use this specialised skill to descend a rock face in a controlled way. Abseiling is also called rappelling and can be used as a rescue technique in an emergency.

KNOW THE ROPES!

Dynamic ropes have a small amount of stretch which make for a softer landing when falling during rock climbing. Static ropes have no stretch, so are better suited for abseiling.

STATIC ROPE

DYNAMIC ROPE

VS

WHAT EQUIPMENT DO I NEED?

To abseil safely, you will need a climbing rope, harness and a belay device. There are different belay devices you can use, but the two most common are called a Figure 8 and an ATC (Air Traffic Controller)

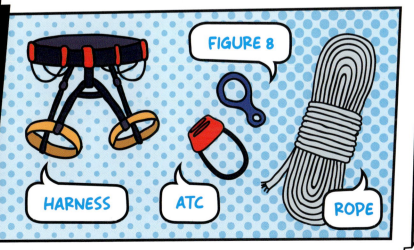

HARNESS

FIGURE 8

ATC

ROPE

WHAT ABOUT ICE CLIMBING?

If you've ever dreamed of climbing up a glittering ice wall surrounded by magical scenery, then here is the sport for you! Ice climbing was born from the pursuit of mountaineering and was just a way to get past an icy section of mountain. Before long, people were scaling icefalls, frozen waterfalls and rock slabs covered with ice and it developed into the extreme sport of ice climbing.

WOW! Did you know you can train all year round at indoor ice climbing walls!

There's no denying – it's a hardcore adventurous sport, a massive workout and a heap of crazy fun!

CAN ANYONE ICE CLIMB?

Ice climbers need a good level of health and fitness, but generally anyone can start ice climbing. Technique and safety are extremely important and there are differences between climbing ice and climbing rock! Specialised guides often lead climbers for their first ice climb.

HOW DO YOU STAY ON THE ICE?

Like rock climbing, climbers are attached to a rope but also carry an ice axe in each hand. Ice climbing boots have metal spikes called crampons that grip into the ice. The first climber or lead climber will fix ice screws for the climbers to attach ropes to as they move upwards, then set up an anchor to safely belay the second climber up.

COOL STUFF

MISSION TO MARS

The world's hardest ice climb is called 'Mission to Mars' at Helmcken Falls in Canada. It is a natural 40-metre ice climb with increasing steepness and a 30-metre overhang!

GRADING SYSTEM

Wow! How does anyone understand all these numbers? Grade systems vary a lot!

They are different between disciplines (bouldering, sport climbing etc.) and vary between geographic regions too.

KNOTS FOR CLIMBING

Knots are cool and fun to learn. You don't have to get too technical, but there are a few essential knots that will keep you out of trouble. Once you know them, you should be able to tie them with your eyes closed!

DOUBLE FIGURE 8

A double figure 8 is the best and safest knot for tying the rope to your harness. It's also super easy to double check, or – better yet – get your partners fresh eyes on it!

GIRTH HITCH

A girth hitch knot is used to tie a sling to your harness or another piece of equipment. It's cool because it can be tied with one hand and is quick and easy to wrangle.

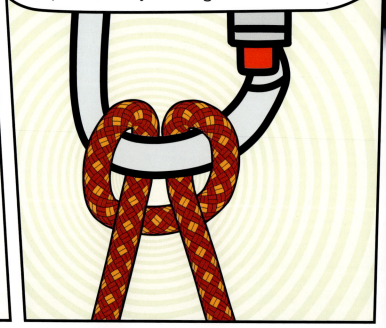

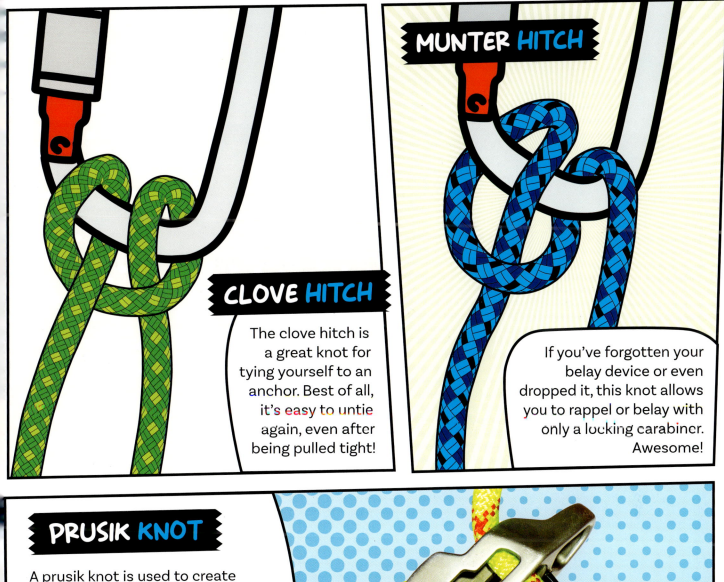

CLOVE HITCH

The clove hitch is a great knot for tying yourself to an anchor. Best of all, it's easy to untie again, even after being pulled tight!

MUNTER HITCH

If you've forgotten your belay device or even dropped it, this knot allows you to rappel or belay with only a locking carabiner. Awesome!

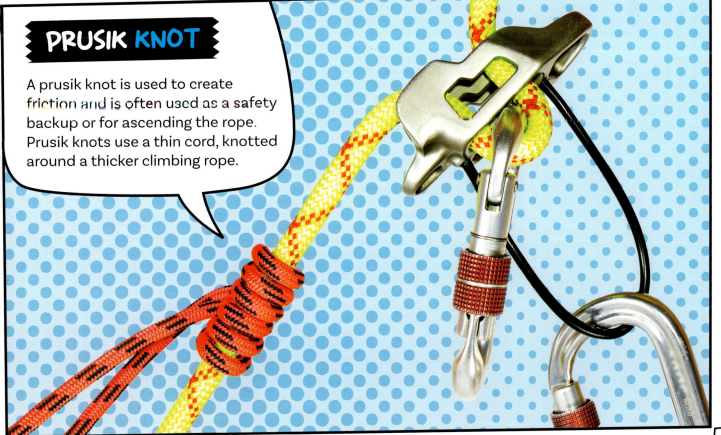

PRUSIK KNOT

A prusik knot is used to create friction and is often used as a safety backup or for ascending the rope. Prusik knots use a thin cord, knotted around a thicker climbing rope.

EXTRA EQUIPMENT AND CLOTHING

Looking good whilst climbing is important, but if your clothes are holding you back, let me give you some tips for being comfortable!

CLOTHING

Freely twisting and bending whilst climbing is critical, so stretchy clothes that allow a full range of motion are essential. Make sure they are hard wearing and reliable. Bruises, scratches and bumps are all part of a great day of climbing, but the right clothes can really soften the beating.

CLIMBING SHOES
The best investment you can make when climbing is in a good pair of climbing shoes. They should fit your feet like a tight glove and be covered with sticky rubber. Sleek, grippy feet mean you can make the best use of tiny footholds and even grip on flat walls with the edges of your feet!

ROPE
Once you have decided you can't live without climbing, you will buy your ropes and look after them with great care. For climbing, you will need a dynamic rope that absorbs impact forces and softens your fall. For abseiling, choose a static rope that will hold your steady descent.

CLIMBING HARNESS
A climbing harness is essential and will save your life if you fall. A good harness will have padding for comfort and gear loops to clip your equipment into.

HARDWARE
Once you start crushing climbs, you will want to get more serious and pick up some quickdraws, carabiners and an ATC. The gear list can be endless, so start with the essentials and add to your kit as you discover how you want to progress.

CHALK
Sweaty, slippery hands are a hard fail on a rock face. Chalk helps to dry the sweat off your hands as you are climbing and makes your skin grippy so you can get good purchase on the rock.

PROFESSIONAL ROCK CLIMBERS

ADAM ONDRA

BORN: 05.02.1993

Adam Ondra is a Czech professional rock climber, currently regarded as the world's best. He specialises in lead climbing and bouldering and has completed the world's hardest climb in Norway. (See page 8)

ES PONTAS, SPAIN

ALEX HONNOLD

BORN: 17.08.1985

Alex Honnold is an American professional rock climber, best known for his free solo ascents of big walls. He is known in particular for his ascent of El Capitan, in Yosemite National Park, in 2017.

EL CAPITAN, USA

CHRIS SHARMA

BORN: 23.04.1981

Born in the USA, Chris Sharma is famous for his lead climbing and deep-water soloing. He is one of the world's best climbers and his signature deep-water solo route is Es Pontas on the Spanish Island of Mallorca.

ALAIN ROBERT

BORN: 07.08.1962

Alain Robert is a French climber also known as 'the French Spiderman'. He is famous for his free solo climbing and for scaling skyscrapers in urban landscapes using no climbing equipment other than some chalk and climbing shoes.

INDOOR ROCK CLIMBING

HOW DOES IT WORK?
Climbing is a fun and challenging sport, and climbing gyms set their routes so there is something for everyone. Colour coded holds are set in a sequence from super easy to ridiculously impossible and everything in-between. It's a great place to connect with the climbing community, build up your strength and have a whole heap of fun in a controlled, safe environment.

Guess what? You don't need to be an athlete with a tonne of gear and experience to climb!

BOULDERING GYMS

There are entire indoor gyms that are just dedicated to bouldering. Bouldering is a type of climbing that doesn't need ropes because the climber stays close to the ground.

Climbers usually traverse a short sequence, with more skilful and powerful moves. A landing mat placed below the boulder will soften your eventual fall or jump. Bouldering gyms are accessible to all and are excellent for skills training, endurance building and shredding up your hands!

IT'S A WORK OF ART!

Modern climbing gyms are works of art! Route setters are people employed to plan and set up carefully graded routes. They use a good mix of holds and obstacles to keep all levels of climbers on their toes.

DANGERS OF THE SPORT

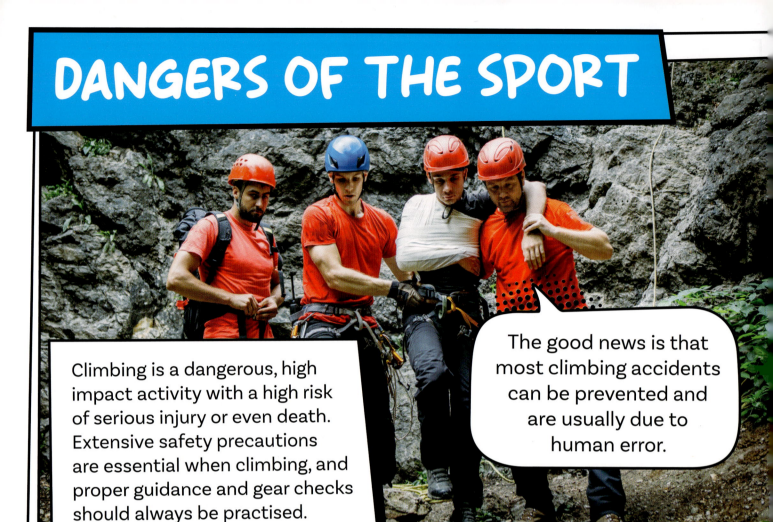

Climbing is a dangerous, high impact activity with a high risk of serious injury or even death. Extensive safety precautions are essential when climbing, and proper guidance and gear checks should always be practised.

The good news is that most climbing accidents can be prevented and are usually due to human error.

HAND INJURIES

If you're a climber or you know one, chances are you will know someone who has had a hand or finger injury.

Rock climbers put excessive load on their hands and fingers which can lead to overuse injuries and shredded, torn up hands - ouch!

FALLING

When lead climbing, if gear placement fails, holds break or a climber gets pumped, this can lead to a dangerous fall. A fall can be awkward, upside-down or even neck-breaking!

RAPPELLING

Rappelling, or abseiling, may seem fairly safe, but if you have a casual attitude, are not paying attention or have not checked your gear properly, it can be extremely dangerous. In serious safety fails, a rappeller can even slip off the end of a too-short rope and die!

ROCK CLIMBING EVENTS

There are competitions, training programs, community events and festivals held all over the world for climbers to take part in the action.

Some of the most important competitions held include:

CLIMBING WORLD CHAMPIONSHIPS

CLIMBING WORLD CUP

SUMMER OLYMPICS

GLOSSARY

ABSEILING — descending a fixed rope down a vertical rockface

ADRENALINE — hormone that helps you react quickly in a stressful situation

BELAY DEVICE — piece of climbing hardware used to control a rope while belaying

BELAYER — person who uses a belay device to control the rope for a climber

BOULDERING — climbing on small rock formations without a rope or harness

CAMS — spring-loaded device that is inserted into rock crevices then expanded to create an anchor point

CARABINERS — metal snap-link used to connect climbing safety systems together

CRAG — rock climbing area, such as a cliff or rock feature

CRAMPONS — metal footwear with spikes that add traction during ice climbing

DEEP-WATER SOLO — free climbing above deep water without a belayer

FREE CLIMBING — climbing without help, but with safety ropes and anchors

FREE SOLOING — climbing without safety devices such as ropes or anchors, but with chalk and climbing shoes

HARNESS — device worn by a climber that a safety rope can attach to

HOLDS — specially formed, shaped grips that are bolted to a climbing wall to form artificial rock formations

ICE AXE — multi-purpose tool used by ice climbers to grip and create holds

ICE CLIMBING — using crampons, picks, ropes and other equipment to climb on ice

ICE SCREW — hollow screw-like device that is screwed into ice to create anchor

LEAD CLIMBER — person who climbs first, in a party of climbers, to create and attach anchors for others to follow

NUTS — metal wedges threaded on a wire, that climbers wedge into rock cracks to create anchor points, also called chocks

OVERHANG — rock formation that exceeds vertical and causes the climber to hang away from the rock

ROUTE SETTERS — people who plan and install artificial climbing wall routes

SPORT CLIMBING — climbing on permanently set routes with pre-set anchors with a rope and belayer

STATIC ROPE — rope that does not stretch, so is good for controlled abseiling

TOP ROPING — climbing using a belayer and top-anchored rope system

TRAD CLIMBING — climbing a route planned and set by yourself, as you go, using carried cams, nuts and chocks

INDEX

ABSEILING	14, 23, 29, 31
BELAY	12, 15, 16, 21, 31
DANGER	19, 28, 29
GRADE	18, 19, 27
GYM	10, 11, 26, 27
ICE	16, 17, 31
KNOTS	20, 21
OLYMPIC	5, 7, 30
TECHNIQUE	10, 14, 16
SAFETY	10, 11, 16, 21, 28, 29, 31
SHOES	10, 12, 23, 25, 26, 31
TOP ROPING	12, 31
TRAD CLIMBING	13, 31